classic british cookbook

This edition printed in 2008 for
Bookmart Ltd
Blaby Road
Wigston
Leicester LE18 4SE

First published in Great Britain in 2005 by
Kyle Cathie Ltd for Sainsbury's Supermarkets Ltd

10 9 8 7 6 5 4 3 2 1

ISBN: 978 1 85626 891 2

Senior editor Helen Woodhall
Designer: Geoff Hayes
Styling: Penny Markham
Home Economist: Annie Nichols
Production: Sha Huxtable and Alice Holloway

With thanks and acknowlegement to all the recipe writers
whose talents have contributed to the creation of this book.

With special thanks to Linda Bain, Nicola Donovan, Amanda
Fries, Sarah Lee and Kate McBain.

Colour reproduction by Scanhouse Pty Ltd
Printed and bound in China by C & C Offset Printers

**The eggs used in this book are medium sized. All spoon
measurements for dry ingredients are heaped. 1 teaspoon =
5ml, 1 tablespoon = 15ml. Always use either metric or
imperial measurements when following a recipe - never
mix the two.**

contents

introduction - the best of british

From the most tender, melting Roast Beef with Yorkshire puddings (page 50) to crunchy, crispy Fish 'n' Chips (page 44), and from seasonal delights such as Asparagus & Spinach Tart to Golden Bramley Pie (page 118), here we bring you the very best of British cooking. Whether it is Scottish salmon (try Roast Salmon with Watercress Sauce, page 46) or the unparalleled range of tasty English cheeses (go for Creamy Celery Soup with Stilton, page 16) - Britain produces some of the world's greatest ingredients. These recipes give suggestions for enjoying them at every stage of a meal.

Soups are delicious and warming - just try our tasty Bacon & Parsnip Soup (page 14). There's

a good range of suggestions for starters, too. Cheese & Mushroom Soufflé (page 28) or succulent Salmon Toasts with Pickled Cucumbers (page 26) will cause a sensation any meal.

As for main courses, try traditional Lincolnshire Sausages with Apples & Mushrooms (page 54) - bangers never go amiss! Beef Wellington with Mushroom & Mustard Sauce (page 48) is great when you've got friends around and want to impress; it really is a glorious party dish. And what could make a finer Sunday roast than Pork with Apple & Celery Stuffing (page 57)?

Who knows who first combined fish with chips? But it's become one of the country's quintessential dishes, newspaper or not! With a huge coastline, plaice and cod, traditionally eaten on Fridays, are Britain's most popular fish, but there's no need to limit yourself to them - there is a fantastic range of seafood out there. Baked Cod with Green Lentils (page 40) or Scallops on a Pea Purée (page 42) make a fabulous fishy feast. Fisherman's Pie (page 36) is another tasty treat if you're in the mood for fish and it is easy to make ahead of time.

Slow cooking produces warming stews with meltingly rich flavours that have cooked for

ours in the oven or in the slowpot cooker
tenderise the meats; we bring you
aditional Lancashire Hotpot (page 62) and
twist on a classic of Cottage Pie with a
arsnip Mash topping (page 66). These
shes are often cooked in one pot only,
hich has the added advantage of making
r less washing up!

here's nothing more simple or seasonal to
ake than Minty Marmalade Lamb with Butter
eans (page 58); it is a welcome variant of
e Sunday roast. Lamb at Eastertime is
articularly special; the new season's lamb
hould just be available.

For vegetarians, there's plenty to choose
from, too. As a light lunch dish, Celery, Pear
& Stilton Crumble Bake (page 90) is difficult
to beat, as are Tangy Roast Roots with
Chestnuts (page 102) – a really filling winter
warmer! Cheesy Kale Gratin (page 84) is a
delicious way to check out what may be an
unfamiliar vegetable.

The humble potato is one of our most
versatile foods – it can be chipped, roasted,
baked, mashed, boiled and made into your
own favourite dish. Try Creamy Mustard
Potato Salad (page 74), Jacket Chips with
Tartar-style Sauce (page 94) or use left-overs

in delicious Bubble & Squeak (page 78).

Although we can now buy a luscious range of fruit and vegetables all year round, there's something very appealing about fresh produce in season. In summer, take advantage of the abundance of grapes, strawberries and blueberries in the beautifully coloured Fresh Fruit Jelly (page 108); it not only looks gorgeous, but tastes so good too. Syllabub is just about as traditionally British as you can get; our Apple Syllabub (page 106) tastes sensational and makes a most refreshing end to the meal. Moving deeper into autumn, when there are plums aplenty on the trees in the

orchards, a Crumble (page 114) is great. When winter bites, Chocolate Bread-and-Butter Pudding (page 122) is comfort food to the extreme and the Apple & Marmalade Custard Pudding (page 116) is sublime. As for seasonal vegetable dishes, Fruity Red Cabbage (page 80) and Spicy Parsnips (page 96) are both delicious and nutritious in cold weather and will have you running back to the pan for more. Bacon & Chestnut Sprouts (page 86) make you realise that Christmas is just around the corner.

Christmas isn't the only festival that has its own special dishes, of course. In Scotland, Burns Night cannot be celebrated without Haggis, Neeps and Tatties (page 52). We've flavoured it with a little Whisky & Mushroom Sauce too! Think of the sound of the bagpipes piping in the festive haggis. In Wales, St David's Day would not be the same without the leek. Try our favourite, Creamed Leeks (page 84). And for Shrove Tuesday, who would go without Pancakes with Lemon (page 110)?

A traditional British skill is baking and for a teatime treat you could get out the flour and make some delicious Spiced Scones (page 112) or even cook up a Parkin (page 121), traditionally eaten on Guy Fawkes' Night.

For centuries cheese has been served at the end of the meal in Britain, especially a

ve meal – could Christmas be complete
out a truckle of Stilton? Cheddar is the
t versatile of our cooking cheeses and
sh Rarebit (page 18) is the most
oursome of dishes – a great stand-by for
oer when you need to be quick. Or try
esy Oat Biscuits with Mackerel Rillettes
ge 22) for a tasty treat.

HOW TO USE THIS BOOK: the chapters are
divided simply into the courses of the meal. We
have given you preparation and cooking time
to help with planning and, as a guide, the
calorie and fat count for each
of the dishes.

starters
and soups

bacon & parsnip soup

Parsnips give a silky texture to this delicious winter warmer.

45 mins		**216** cals	**15g** fat
prep & cook time	serves 6	per serving	per serving

25g (1oz) butter
1 tablespoon oil
1 onion, chopped
1 carrot, peeled and chopped
250g (8oz) parsnips, chopped
250g (8oz) cooked lean gammon or shoulder
　　joint, cut into 1cm (1/2in) dice
1 litre (1³/4 pints) vegetable stock
croutons to serve
single cream, to serve
1 tablespoon freshly chopped parsley
freshly ground black pepper

Heat the butter and oil in a large pan. Add the onion, carrot and parsnip and cook gently for 5-6 minutes until softened but not browned. Add the gammon and stock and bring to the boil. Simmer for 25-30 minutes until the vegetables are soft.

Purée the soup in a blender until smooth and return to the pan. You may have to do this in batches. Add pepper to taste (the gammon is fairly salty, so you will not need to add extra salt in the cooking) and serve hot with croûtons, a swirl of cream and freshly chopped parsley.

creamy celery soup with stilton

Tangy cheese gives real bite and body to this tasty soup.

45 mins — prep & cook time

serves 6

197 cals — per serving

12g fat — per serving

1 tablespoon olive oil
1 onion, finely chopped
2 large potatoes, peeled and diced
1 head celery, thoroughly washed and
    roughly chopped
1 teaspoon caraway seeds
1 vegetable stock cube made up with 600ml
    (1 pint) boiling water
300ml (¹/₂ pint) semi-skimmed milk
150ml (¹/₄ pint) single cream
75g (3oz) Stilton cheese, crumbled
20g (³/₄oz) fresh chives, roughly chopped

Heat the oil in a large saucepan then add the onion, potato, celery and caraway seeds. Fry gently for approximately 5 minutes until the onion is softened but not browned.

Add the stock and milk and simmer uncovered for 20-30 minutes. Transfer the soup in batches to a food processor and process until smooth, then return to the rinsed saucepan.

Gently reheat the soup, then stir in the single cream. Do not allow to boil. Crumble the Stilton cheese into individual soup bowls and pour over the soup. Sprinkle with chives and serve immediately with hot crusty bread.

quick welsh rarebit

Classic comfort food - the
ultimate cheese on toast!

20 mins
prep & cook
time

serves 4

303 cals
per
serving

21g fat
per
serving

4 large slices of bread
25g (1oz) butter, at room temperature
1 teaspoon English mustard
¹/₂ teaspoon Worcestershire sauce
175g (6oz) Davidstow or any well-flavoured
Cheddar cheese, grated
2 tablespoons milk
salt and freshly ground black pepper

Preheat a grill and toast the bread on one side.

Meanwhile, mix together the softened butter, the
mustard, salt and freshly ground black pepper,
Worcestershire sauce, cheese and milk.

Spread the mixture over the untoasted sides of
the bread and brown under the hot grill for 2-3
minutes. Serve immediately.

COOK'S TIPS
A good quality Cheddar is essential for this
recipe. Cheaper cheese will give a stringy, oily
result, so splash out on the best!

You can also use the topping on fish, chicken
or pork.

glamorgan sausages

Meat-free bangers – a traditional favourite given a modern twist.

30 mins		**160** cals	**11**g fat
prep & cook time	serves 8	per serving	per serving

25g (1oz) butter
1 large onion, finely chopped
250g (8oz) fresh white breadcrumbs
1/2 teaspoon dry mustard powder
2 tablespoons freshly chopped parsley
100g (3 1/2oz) Welsh cheese such as Caerphilly,
    Y Fenni or Tintern, crumbled or grated
2 large eggs, beaten
2 tablespoons plain flour
2 tablespoons vegetable oil
salt and freshly ground black pepper

Melt the butter in a small frying pan and gently fry the onion for 3-4 minutes until it has just softened. Transfer to a bowl and mix with the breadcrumbs, mustard, parsley, cheese and good sprinkling of seasoning.

Bind the mixture together with the beaten eggs. Divide into eight and form into sausage shapes or small patties. Lightly roll in the flour.

Heat the oil in a frying pan and gently fry the 'sausages' or cakes for 3-4 minutes on each side until golden brown.

Drain on kitchen paper and serve immediately, with a relish or pickle and a green salad.

cheesy oat cakes with mackerel rillettes

The fresher the mackerel, the better the flavours of this rich starter will be.

prep & cook time | serves 6 | **787** cals per serving | **66**g fat per serving

For the cheesy oatcakes:
75g (3oz) Scottish porridge oats
150g (5oz) plain flour
100g (3½oz) unsalted butter, cut into 1cm (½in) dice
75g (3oz) Parmesan cheese, grated
50g (2oz) Cheddar cheese, grated
2 egg yolks
cold water

For the mackerel rillettes:
250g (8oz) smoked mackerel fillets, skin removed and flaked
250ml (8fl oz) crème fraîche
1 teaspoon horseradish sauce
20g (¾oz) fresh parsley, finely chopped
salt and freshly ground black pepper

Preheat the oven to 200°C/400°F/gas mark 6.

To make the oatcakes, combine the oats and flour In a large bowl , then rub in the butter. Add the cheeses and mix to a dough with the egg yolks and approximately 4 tablespoons cold water. Leave to rest for 30 minutes.

On a lightly floured surface roll out to 1cm (½in) thick, then cut out circles using a 7cm (2½in) pastry cutter. Transfer to a baking sheet and cook for 10-15 minutes or until golden brown.

Transfer to a cooling rack to cool.

To make the mackerel rillettes, combine all the ingredients in a large bowl and mash with a fo until thoroughly mixed.

Press spoonfuls of the mackerel mixture between two spoons. Serve with 2 biscuits and sprig of parsley.

Rillettes is the French name for a rough pât made by flaking fish or meat and mixing it with cream or butter. Rillettes are commonly made with pork, duck or rabbit.

Although this is quite a high-fat dish, don't it put you off. Eating just one portion of oily fish a week has been shown to be good for your health as it contains omega-3 fatty acids, which protect against heart disease, stroke or arthritis.

quick kedgeree

Adapted by the Victorians from a traditional Indian recipe, kedgeree makes a great alternative to the great British fry-up for breakfast.

45 mins | **383 cals** | **11g fat**

prep & cook time   serves 4   per serving   per serving

250g (8oz) smoked cod loin, skinned and boned

500g (1lb) cooked long-grain rice or 125g (4oz) raw long grain rice, cooked as per pack instructions and refreshed in cold water

500g (1lb) jar korma curry cooking sauce

75g (3oz) frozen peas

2 eggs, hard-boiled, shelled and cut into quarters

20g (³/₄oz) flat-leaf parsley, finely chopped

Poach the fish in a large pan of simmering water for 5–10 minutes until just cooked through, then flake into large pieces.

Place the rice in a medium-size saucepan then add the korma sauce and cook over a moderate heat for 5 minutes. Add the peas and fish and cook for a further 2–3 minutes.

Pile onto individual serving plates and finish with the quartered egg and a scattering of parsley.

salmon toasts with pickled cucumber

A beautifully fresh and simple starter or easy light lunch.

2½ hrs		225 cals	4g fat
prep & cook time	serves 4	per serving	per serving

4 slices from an uncut malted grain loaf
1 cucumber, halved and deseeded
juice of ½ lemon
2 tablespoons sugar
250g (8oz) smoked Scottish salmon, cut into strips

Preheat the grill to a moderate heat.

Place the bread slices under the grill and cook until golden on both sides. Remove the crusts, cut the slices in half vertically, then cut into triangles. Place back under the grill and cook until golden and slightly curled. Put to one side to cool.

Next grate the cucumber and place in a bowl with the lemon juice and sugar. Mix to combine then leave to pickle for 2 hours.

To serve, arrange 4 pieces of toast on each plate, then top with some smoked salmon, followed by some pickled cucumber. Drizzle some of the cucumber pickling juice around the edge of the plate. Serve immediately.

cheese and mushroom soufflé

Originally a French dish, soufflé has become a firm British favourite. Here it's given extra bite with mature Cheddar cheese and English mustard.

1 hour	serves 4	300 cals	21g fat
prep & cook time	serves 4	per serving	per serving

50g (2oz) butter
40g (1½oz) plain flour
300ml (½ pint) milk
4 eggs, separated
75g (3oz) mature Cheddar cheese, grated
50g (2oz) button mushrooms, sliced
1 tablespoon freshly chopped chives
¼ teaspoon English mustard
salt and freshly ground black pepper

Preheat the oven to 180°C/350°F/gas mark 4. Lightly oil a 1.2 litre (2 pint) soufflé dish.

Melt the butter in a large saucepan, stir in the flour and cook for 1 minute. Remove from the heat and gradually whisk in the milk. Return to the heat and bring to the boil, stirring continuously until the sauce thickens. Beat in the egg yolks, cheese, mushrooms, chives, mustard and season to taste.

Whisk the egg whites until stiff, then fold a quarter into the cheese mixture, followed by the remainder. Spoon into the soufflé dish and bake in the preheated oven for 35–40 minutes until risen and golden brown. Serve immediately.

tart of black pudding, smoked bacon and caramelised onion

An indulgence based on one of our oldest traditional dishes. The best black pudding comes from Yorkshire.

1½ hrs		858 cals	60g fat
prep & cook time	serves 4	per serving	per serving

500g (1lb) puff pastry
flour for dusting
1 tablespoon olive oil
2 red onions, sliced
2 teaspoons double cream
250g (8oz) chestnut mushrooms, quartered and cooked
4 rashers rindless smoked back bacon, grilled
250g (8oz) black pudding, sliced and quickly fried
125g (4oz) mixed herb salad
1 teaspoon lemon oil
drizzle of good, aged balsamic vinegar
salt and freshly ground black pepper

Preheat the oven to 200°C/400°F/gas mark 6. Lightly grease a baking sheet.

Roll out the puff pastry on a lightly floured work surface until large enough to cut out 4 discs of pastry, 15cm (6in) in diameter. Allow the pastry discs to rest for 5 minutes.

Prick the pastry all over with a fork. Place on the baking sheet and cook in the preheated oven for approximately 10 minutes or until golden. Remove and cool.

Reduce the oven temperature to 190°C/375°F/gas mark 5.

Heat the olive oil in a saucepan, add the onion and cook slowly for approximately 25 minutes until lightly caramelised. Add the cream and cook for a further 5 minutes. Season with salt and freshly ground black pepper.

To assemble the tart spread the onion mix on the pastry, top with the mushrooms, bacon and slice of fried black pudding.

Bake in the oven for 10 minutes.

Mix the salad with the lemon oil and season. Place the tart and salad on a plate and drizzle with balsamic vinegar. Serve immediately.

main
courses

asparagus and spinach tart

A tasty take on a British favourite.

60 mins
prep & cook time

serves 8-10

493 cals
per serving

34g fat
per serving

500g (1lb) ready-rolled shortcrust pastry
2 large potatoes
125g (4oz) fine asparagus
1 teaspoon smoked ground paprika
50g (2oz) Cheddar cheese, grated
250g (8oz) spinach
3 eggs, lightly beaten
200ml (7fl oz) double cream
salt and freshly ground black pepper

Preheat the oven to 180°C/350°F/gas mark 4.
Grease a 28cm (11in) fluted flan tin at least 4cm
(1½in) deep.

Roll out the pastry and use it to line the flan tin.
Lightly prick the base all over and refrigerate for
30 minutes.

Place a piece of baking parchment over the
pastry, cover evenly with uncooked rice or
baking beans and bake blind for 15 minutes.
Remove the parchment and rice and continue
baking for a further 5 minutes until golden.

Cook the potatoes whole in boiling water for 20
minutes or until they are tender, then refresh
under cold water, peel and slice.

Meanwhile cook the asparagus stems in boiling
water for 2 minutes. Remove and refresh under
cold, running water.

Place a layer of potato, a pinch of paprika,
seasoning and a sprinkling of Cheddar in the
pastry case. Add a layer of spinach, a pinch of
paprika, seasoning and a sprinkling of Cheddar.
Repeat the layers.

Whisk the eggs and cream together, and pour
over the filling, reserving a little. Arrange a line
of cooked asparagus over the top and pour the
rest of the egg mixture over the top. Bake for
20-25 minutes until golden.

COOK'S TIP
Buy the best quality Cheddar cheese that
you can afford for this recipe - poor quality
cheese has a tendency to turn oily and
stringy when cooked.

fisherman's pie

You can ring the changes with many different types of fish; equall•
it is fun to try different potato toppings.

prep & cook time   serves 4   290 cals per serving   4g fat per serving

1 large potato, scrubbed and thinly sliced
250g (8oz) coley fillets
250g (8oz) cod fillets
2 sticks celery, trimmed and sliced
75g (3oz) mushrooms, wiped and sliced
1 medium leek, trimmed and sliced
300ml (½ pint) fish stock, or other home-
    made stock
2 tablespoons cornflour
200ml (7fl oz) skimmed milk
2 teaspoons English mustard
50g (2oz) canned or frozen sweetcorn
2 tablespoons freshly chopped chives
    or 1 tablespoon dried chives
2 medium tomatoes, thinly sliced
50g (2oz) reduced-fat Cheddar cheese, grated

Preheat oven to 200°C/400°F/gas mark 6.

Place the potato slices in a saucepan and cover
with water. Bring to the boil and cook for 4-5
minutes until tender. Drain well and set aside.

Wash the fish and place in a frying pan. Add the
celery, mushrooms and leek. Pour over the stock,
bring to the boil, cover and simmer for 5-6
minutes until the fish is tender.

Drain the fish and vegetables, reserving 75ml
(3fl oz) of the cooking liquid. Discard the skin fr•
the fish, and flake into bite-sized pieces. Set asi•
Blend the cornflour with 4 tablespoons of the
milk to form a paste. Pour the remaining milk
into a saucepan with the reserved cooking liqu•
Stir in the cornflour paste. Bring to the boil,
stirring, until thickened.

Remove from the heat and stir in the fish,
vegetables, mustard, sweetcorn and chives.
Mix well and pile into the base of an ovenproo•
pie dish.

Arrange the sliced tomatoes on top, then the
sliced potato. Sprinkle with Cheddar cheese an•
bake in the oven for 20-25 minutes until golde•

COOK'S TIP
Adapt to use whatever fish you have availab•
- you can add cooked shelled prawns, salmo•
or even a tin of tuna according to your taste

vegetable puff pie

Mushrooms, leek, broccoli and cheese make this hearty pie a meal in itself.

prep & cook time   **serves 4**   **567 cals** per serving   **38g fat** per serving

50g (2oz) butter
40g (1¹/₂oz) plain flour
450ml (³/₄ pint) milk
125g (4oz) grated Cheddar cheese
1 tablespoon freshly chopped parsley
pinch of English mustard powder
125g (4oz) button mushrooms, halved and
     sautéed
1 carrot, sliced
1 leek, sliced and blanched
75g (3oz) broccoli florets, blanched
250g (8oz) ready-to-roll puff pastry
beaten egg or milk to glaze
salt and freshly ground black pepper

Preheat the oven to 200°C/400°F/gas mark 6.

Melt the butter in a saucepan, add the flour and cook for 1 minute. Remove from the heat and gradually whisk in the milk. Return to the heat and bring to the boil, stirring continuously until the sauce thickens. Stir in the cheese, parsley and mustard.

Add the mushrooms, carrot, leek, broccoli, and seasoning to taste. Mix well and place in a lightly oiled pie dish.

Dampen the pie dish rim. Roll out the pastry on a lightly floured surface. Cut off a strip of pastry and place on the rim of the dish and brush it with water.

Lay the pastry lid over the top and press the edges together to seal. Trim and flute the edges. Make a hole in the top of the pie to let out the air whilst cooking, and use the trimmings to decorate the pie. Glaze well.

Place in the preheated oven for 30 minutes until golden brown.

baked cod with green lentils

The taste and texture of cod are what makes this fish so popular.

prep & cook time   serves 4   per serving   per serving

300g (10oz) Anya potatoes, quartered
1 x 410g (13oz) can green lentils, drained and rinsed
oil, for brushing and to oil baking tray
1 tablespoon Dijon mustard
50g (2oz) butter, melted
2 fresh rosemary sprigs
625g (1¹/₄lb) boneless cod loin, skinned and cut into 4 portions
1 tablespoon yellow mustard seeds
50g (2oz) butter
2 tablespoons flat-leaf parsley, chopped
salt and freshly ground black pepper

Preheat the oven to 180°C/350°F/gas mark 4. Lightly oil a baking tray.

Simmer the potatoes in lightly salted water for 5 minutes until just tender. Drain well.

Put the potatoes and lentils on the baking tray. Mix the Dijon mustard, melted butter and rosemary together and drizzle over. Season well. Place the cod portions on top. Bake for 20 minutes or until the fish is cooked through.

Place the mustard seeds in a small saucepan, crush with the end of a rolling pin, and stir ove a low heat until aromatic – about 30 seconds. Add the butter to the pan, melt and stir in the flat-leaf parsley. Season well.

Serve the cod, potatoes and lentils immediatel with the mustard seed mixture poured over.

COOK'S TIP
Be careful not to overcook the cod or it will be dry and tasteless.

scallops on pea purée

A real treat. The freshest scallops still smell of the sea!

30 mins		**382** cals	**27**g fat
prep & cook time	serves 4	per serving	per serving

½ small onion, chopped
25g (1oz) butter
250g (8oz) peas
dash of white wine
2 teaspoons chervil
2 teaspoons tarragon
1 tablespoon double cream
12 large scallops
butter for frying
deep-fried shredded leek to garnish (optional)
salt and freshly ground black pepper

Fry the onion in the butter for 5 minutes until softened but not browned. Add the peas and a dash of white wine and leave to bubble for 5–10 minutes.

Season and stir in the chervil, tarragon and cream. Purée until smooth.

Pan-fry the scallops in butter over a high heat. for 1–2 minutes each side. Be careful not to overcook or they will be unpleasantly rubbery in the texture.

To serve, place a ring of purée on each plate, top with scallops and garnish with a pile of deep-fried shredded leek.

fish and chips with minted mushy peas

A delicious version of the chip-shop classic.

1½ hrs prep & cook time   serves 6   **506 cals** per serving   **11g fat** per serving

For the batter:
15g (³/₄oz) fresh yeast or 7g (¹/₂oz) sachet
    of dried yeast
300ml (¹/₂ pint) strong ale, such as Bishop's
    Finger
250g (8oz) plain flour
1 teaspoon salt
2 teaspoons mustard seeds

4 x skinless, boneless cod fillets
    (each approximately 125g (4oz) in weight)
oil for deep frying

750g (1¹/₂lb) potatoes, peeled and cut into
    chips

1 x 300g (10oz) tin mushy peas
1 tablespoon crème fraîche
20g (³/₄oz) fresh mint, finely chopped
salt and freshly ground black pepper

If using fresh yeast, cream it with a little of the
ale so it becomes liquid. If using dried yeast add
it to the flour. Sift the flour and salt into a large
bowl, make a well in the centre and pour in the
remaining ale and yeast mix. Slowly mix together,
gradually incorporating the flour into the liquid.
Whisk until smooth, then add the mustard seeds
and freshly ground black pepper. Leave to prove
for 1 hour.

Preheat the deep fat fryer to 190°C/375°F.

Dip the fish into the batter. Deep fry for 5
minutes or until golden brown and crisp, then
drain on kitchen paper. Repeat the process for
the remaining fish. Keep the cooked fish warm
in the oven.

Cook the chips in batches for 5 minutes or until
golden brown. In the meantime heat the mushy
peas as per tin instructions, then stir in the
crème fraîche and mint. Serve the fish along
with the chips and mushy peas.

roast salmon with watercress sauce

A peppery watercress sauce cuts through the richness of salmon in a great combination of flavours.

30 mins	serves 4	728 cals	60g fat
prep & cook time	serves 4	per serving	per serving

100ml (3¹/₂fl oz) dry white wine
300ml (¹/₂ pint) fish stock
284ml (10fl oz) double cream
75g (3oz) watercress, washed
1 tablespoon vegetable oil
4 x 200g (7oz) salmon fillets
salt and freshly ground black pepper

Preheat the oven to 220°C/425°F/gas mark 7.

Pour the wine and the fish stock into a medium saucepan, bring to the boil and reduce by half. Add the double cream and bring to the boil. Add the watercress and cook for 1–2 minutes, seasoning to taste. Remove from the heat.

Pour into a liquidiser or food processor and blend until smooth. Then return the sauce to a clean saucepan.

To cook the salmon, heat a non-stick frying pan, add the oil and place the salmon skin-side down in the pan for 2 minutes over a medium heat. Transfer the salmon to a baking sheet and place in the oven for 8–10 minutes, until just cooked. Remove from the oven and reheat the sauce.

Serve with the watercress sauce and a tomato and shallot salad.

beef wellington with mushroom and mustard sauce

Perfect for special occasions, these individual beef Wellingtons are quite delicious.

1 hr	serves 2	1080 cals	69g fat
prep & cook time	serves 2	per serving	per serving

1 tablespoon olive oil
25g (1oz) butter
2 x 125g (4oz) pieces fillet steak
1 red onion, finely diced
125g (4oz) button mushrooms, diced
2 teaspoons wholegrain mustard
2 tablespoons dry sherry
375g (12oz) ready-to-roll puff pastry, defrosted
1 egg, beaten, to glaze
150ml (¼ pint) red wine
2 tablespoons single cream
salt and freshly ground black pepper

Preheat the oven to 220°C/425°F/gas mark 7.

Heat the oil and butter in a frying pan and quickly seal the steaks on both sides. Remove from the pan and allow to cool.

Add the onion and mushrooms to the pan and cook for 6-8 minutes, stirring occasionally. Stir in the mustard, sherry and seasoning, cook for a further 2 minutes and allow to cool.

On a lightly floured surface, cut the pastry in half and roll out one piece large enough to 'wrap' around one steak. Place a heaped teaspoon of the mushroom mixture in the centre of the pastry, top with the beef and place a further spoonful of the mixture on the beef.

Brush the edges of the pastry with water and with a sharp knife make cuts in from the corne Wrap the pastry around the meat to seal completely and place seal-side down on a baki tray. Repeat with the other steak.

Make pastry leaves with any remaining pastry and stick on top with a little water. Brush with beaten egg and bake in the preheated oven for 20-25 minutes until risen and golden brown.

To make the sauce, add the wine to the remaining mushroom mixture and reduce slightly. Stir in the cream and serve hot with the beef.

roast beef with yorkshire pudding & gravy

The classic Sunday roast cooked to perfection; the meat has more flavour if cooked on the bone.

2 hrs — prep & cook time

serves 4

539 cals — per serving

30g fat — per serving

600-900g (1½-2lb) beef topside
25g (1oz) beef dripping
1 tablespoon ready-made mustard, to taste

For the Yorkshire puddings:
125g (4oz) plain flour, sifted
½ teaspoon salt
1 egg
200ml (7fl oz) milk
75ml (3fl oz) water

1 tablespoon plain flour
2 tablespoons water
300ml (10fl oz) beef stock
salt and freshly ground black pepper

Preheat the oven to 200°C/400°F/gas mark 6.

Place the beef on a rack in a roasting tin. Then add the dripping, and rub in some seasoning and mustard to taste.

Cook the beef for 20 minutes per 500g (1lb), plus 20 minutes, if you like your beef rare; 25 minutes per 500g (1lb), plus 25 minutes, if you like your beef medium; and 30 minutes per 500g (1lb), plus 30 minutes, if you like it well done.

To make the Yorkshire pudding, mix the flour and salt together, then add the egg and half the milk. Beat until smooth and add the remaining milk and water.

Forty minutes before the meat is cooked, drain off all but 2 large spoonfuls of the juices into a Yorkshire pudding tin. Pour the Yorkshire pudding batter into the tin and return to the oven. Increase the oven temperature to 220°C/425°F/gas mark 7.

When the meat is cooked, remove from the oven and leave to rest for 10 minutes. Allow the Yorkshire puddings to cook for a further 10 minutes until just cooked.

To make the gravy, skim the fat off the juices in the roasting tin and bring the juices to the boil. Blend the flour with the water and stir in. Cook for 2-3 minutes, then add the beef stock to reach the required consistency, and season to taste. Simmer gently for a further 2-3 minutes and serve.

When selecting a joint of beef for a Sunday roast, allow 175g (6oz) per person off the bone or 225g (8oz) on the bone.

haggis with whisky and mushroom sauce, and neep and tatty mash

Celebrate Burns Night with this traditional feast!

45 mins
prep & cook time

serves 4-6

539 cals
per serving

30g fat
per serving

1 x 450g (15oz) haggis
1 tablespoon oil
150g (5oz) button mushrooms, sliced
150ml (¼ pint) chicken stock
1 teaspoon cornflour blended with 1-2
   tablespoons whisky
1 swede (England) or turnip (Scotland)
   weighing approximately 875g (1¾lb),
   peeled and diced
1kg (2lb) potatoes eg King Edward, cut into
   large chunks
50g (2oz) butter
4 tablespoons cream or yogurt
green beans or other green vegetable to serve
salt and freshly ground black pepper

Cook the haggis following all the instructions on the pack.

Heat the oil in a saucepan and cook the mushrooms for 8-10 minutes until softened and golden. Add the stock and cornflour blended with the whisky. Bring to the boil and simmer for 2-3 minutes until thickened and smooth. Season to taste.

Meanwhile, cook the swede (turnip) and potato together or separately in slightly salted boiling water for 20 minutes or until tender.

Drain the swede (turnip) and potatoes and mash together with the butter and cream or yogurt and plenty of seasoning to taste.

Serve the haggis with the sauce poured over with the neep and tatty mash and green beans.

lincolnshire sausages with apples and mushrooms

The great British banger served on a bed of fluffy mash. Perfect!

30 mins | **serves 4** | **639 cals** | **47g fat**
prep & cook time | serves 4 | per serving | per serving

300ml (½ pint) dry white wine
450g (15oz) Lincolnshire sausages
50g (2oz) butter
1 onion, grated
2 green crisp apples, peeled, cored and sliced
150g (5oz) button mushrooms, wiped and
  halved
200ml (7fl oz) vegetable stock
2 tablespoons unrefined dark brown soft sugar
½ teaspoon ground cinnamon

Bring the wine to the boil in a large frying pan and cook the sausages for 10 minutes. Remove the sausages from the pan, discarding the skins and leaving the wine in the pan.

Heat half the butter in another frying pan and cook the sausages for 10 minutes, until golden brown. Add the onion to the white wine along with the apples, mushrooms, stock, sugar, cinnamon and remaining butter. Bring the mixture to the boil and cook until the apples are tender and the liquid is reduced to a thin syrup.

Serve the sausages with the apple sauce on a bed of mashed potato.

roast pork with apple and celery stuffing

The classic combination of pork and apples – too good to save for Sundays.

 2 hrs   **318** cals   **10g** fat

prep & cook time   serves 6   per serving   per serving

1.25kg (3lb) boneless leg of pork
75g (3oz) wholemeal breadcrumbs
2 sticks celery, finely chopped, leaves
   reserved
1 small onion, grated
1 small cooking apple, finely chopped
40g (1¹/₂oz) chopped hazelnuts
2 tablespoons freshly chopped sage or thyme
1 egg
salt and freshly ground black pepper

Preheat the oven to 160°C/325°F/gas mark 3.

Remove the skin and a thin layer of the fat from the pork. Score the remaining fat with a sharp knife to make a diamond pattern.

Place all the remaining ingredients in a bowl and mix well. Open out the pork and spread the stuffing over it, roll it up and tie with string. Place on a rack in a roasting tin and season to taste. Roast for approximately 2 hours, basting occasionally.

Serve garnished with celery leaves. Skim off and discard any fat from the juices and serve as gravy.

minty marmalade lamb with butter beans

A marmalade glaze gives a fruity twist to this traditionally English roast.

2 hrs		381 cals	16g fat
prep & cook time	serves 4-6	per serving	per serving

1 x 750g (1³/₄lb) prime roasting lamb leg joint
3 tablespoons marmalade
1 tablespoon mint sauce
2 x 410g (14oz) cans butter beans, drained and rinsed

Preheat the oven to 190°C/375°F/gas mark 5.

Place the lamb joint in a roasting tin and cook for 1-1¹/₂ hours, depending on how rare you like it.

In a bowl combine the marmalade and mint, then use it to glaze the lamb 15 minutes before the cooking time is complete.

Five minutes before the end of the cooking time, add the butter beans to the roasting tin and baste with the lamb juices.

To serve, pile the beans and pan juices onto individual plates and top with slices of lamb.

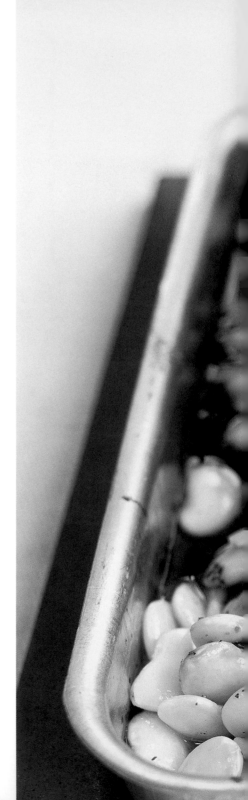

slow-cooked steak in stout

A rich, hearty supper dish, slow-cooked to
release all the flavours.

2 hrs		318 cals	11g fat
prep & cook time	serves 5	per serving	per serving

1 tablespoon oil
750g (1³/4lb) braising steak, trimmed of
   any fat and cut into cubes
2 onions, finely sliced
500g (1lb) root vegetables such as carrots,
   parsnips and swede, diced
2 x 330ml (11fl oz) bottles stout
450ml (³/4 pint) beef stock
250g (8oz) button mushrooms, sliced
3 bay leaves
2 tablespoons redcurrant jelly
1 teaspoon wholegrain mustard
1 tablespoon cornflour, blended with a little
   cold water
1 tablespoon freshly chopped thyme
salt and freshly ground black pepper

Heat the oil in a large flameproof casserole dish,
add half the steak, quickly cook until browned on
all sides and then remove from the pan. Add the
remaining meat and brown in the same way.

Return all the meat to the pan with the onions
and root vegetables. Add the stout, stock,
mushrooms and bay leaves. Bring to the boil
then cover and simmer gently for 1½ hours, until
the meat is tender.

Stir in the redcurrant jelly and mustard. Stir in
the blended cornflour and thyme, bring to the
boil, then reduce the heat and cook for a further
2-3 minutes until thickened and glossy. Season
to taste and garnish with a little more chopped
thyme if desired.

Delicious served with mashed potatoes mixed
with a tablespoonful of creamed horseradish.

lancashire hotpot

An excellent stew traditionally served with pickled red cabbage.

2 hrs	**serves 4**	**565 cals**	**26g fat**
prep & cook time		per serving	per serving

1kg (2lb) potatoes
500g (1lb) scrag and middle neck lamb
125g (4oz) lambs' kidneys, skinned, halved and cored
1 large onion, sliced
1 large carrot, sliced
300ml (1/2 pint) boiling water
20g (3/4oz) margarine or dripping, melted
1 sprig chopped parsley to garnish
salt and freshly ground black pepper

Preheat the oven to 190°C/375°F/gas mark 5. Grease a 1.5 litre (2½ pint) deep casserole.

Halve enough potatoes to make a layer on top of the dish and set aside. Slice the rest thickly and put in the casserole. Cover with the scrag and neck of lamb, lambs' kidneys, onion and carrot, seasoning each layer with salt and pepper to taste. Pour in the boiling water. Cover with the reserved potatoes and brush with the melted fat.

Cover and cook in the preheated oven for 2 hours, removing the lid after 1 hour to brown the potatoes. Garnish with the chopped parsley.

Serve with a green vegetable.

cornish pasties

The original food to go, the earliest Cornish pasties were baked with meat at one end and fruit at the other.

prep & cook time | serves 4 | per serving | per serving

450g (15oz) shortcrust pastry, made with lard
450g (15oz) pie beef: rump or chuck steak or skirt
100g (3½oz) onions, chopped finely
75g (3oz) yellow swede, diced
250g (8oz) potato, diced
1 egg, beaten, to glaze
salt and freshly ground black pepper

Preheat the oven to 200°C/400°F/gas mark 6.

Roll out the pastry and cut into four discs, using side plates as markers for the shape. Chill while you prepare the filling.

Cut away all the skin and gristle from the meat, then chop into a small dice. Season.

Take the beef, onions, swede and potato and place in layers on one half of each pastry disc. Brush the edges with the beaten egg, fold the other half of the pastry disc over the filling to give it a half-moon shape and twist the edges or pinch together to seal the pastry and give it its characteristic rope-like, zig-zag finish.

Make 2 small steam holes in the top of each pasty and brush with the rest of the egg glaze. Bake for 10 minutes, then lower the temperature to 180°C/350°F/gas mark 4, and bake for a further 40 minutes.

Cover with foil if they seem to be browning too fast. Serve warm or cold.

cottage pie with parsnip mash topping

A real family favourite topped with crunchy golden potato.

1 hr
prep & cook time

serves 6

258 cals
per serving

13g fat
per serving

1 tablespoon oil
500g (1lb) extra lean minced beef
1 onion, chopped
2 carrots, peeled and finely chopped
1 x 400g (14oz) can chopped tomatoes
200ml (7fl oz) beef stock
1 tablespoon tomato purée
750g (1³/₄lb) parsnips, peeled and quartered
4 tablespoons milk
25g (1oz) butter or margarine
1 tablespoon chopped flat-leaf parsley
   (optional)
salt and freshly ground black pepper

Preheat the oven to 200°C/400°F/gas mark 6.

Heat the oil in a saucepan, add the beef, onion and carrot and cook for 6-8 minutes, stirring occasionally until evenly browned.

Stir in the tomatoes, stock and tomato purée and simmer for 20-25 minutes, stirring occasionally, until the meat is tender. Add seasoning to taste.

Meanwhile, cook the parsnips in lightly salted boiling water for 15 minutes or until tender. D and mash with the milk, butter or margarine liberal quantities of seasoning.

Spoon the meat mixture into an ovenproof dis and top with the mashed parsnips. Place in th preheated oven for 20-25 minutes, until the topping is golden.

Delicious served with green vegetables.

pork pie

Another favourite with a long history. The first recorded recipe for a pork pie dates back to 1390.

2½ hrs		**516** cals	**27**g fat
prep & cook time	serves 6-8	per serving	per serving

375g (12oz) plain flour
1 teaspoon salt
150ml (¼ pint) water
125g (4oz) lard, cut into small pieces

1kg (2lb) minced lean pork
50g (2oz) onion, very finely chopped
150ml (¼ pint) dry white wine, plus extra
2 tablespoons cognac
½ teaspoon dried sage or thyme
1 generous tablespoon Dijon mustard
1 small eating apple, peeled and grated
  coarsely
1 teaspoon salt
freshly ground black pepper

1 beaten egg, to glaze

1 packet of aspic powder

You will need a 15cm (6in) round, loose-based cake tin.

To make the pastry: sieve the flour with the salt and make a well in the centre. Heat the water with the lard until the lard has melted; pour this mixture into the flour. Mix to a soft dough and knead until smooth. Keep warm and covered, or it will dry out.

Preheat the oven to 200°C/400°F/gas mark 6

Mix the minced pork with the onion, wine, cognac, herbs, mustard, apple and seasoning.

Line the cake tin with three-quarters of the pastry (keep the remainder wrapped in cling film in a warm place). Pack the lined tin with the meat mixture; roll out the remaining pastry and fit the lid. Make a hole in the lid and pull back the edges.

Decorate and glaze the pie with beaten egg, and then put on a baking tray in the oven and bake for 30 minutes.

Reduce the oven temperature to 180°C/ 350°F/gas mark 4 and continue cooking for a further 1½ hours.

When the cooked pie has cooled, make up the aspic jelly with half the recommended liquid (use white wine rather than water for extra flavour if you prefer). Pour it through the hole in the lid, slowly and in stages, until the pie will absorb no more.

Once the aspic has set, wrap the pie and store for a couple of days before cutting it. Serve cold with salad.

side dishes

nutty coleslaw salad

American in origin, coleslaw has become an essential part of a British salad spread.

30 mins
prep & cook time

serves 6

115 cals
per serving

5g fat
per serving

½ small white cabbage, shredded
2 carrots, peeled and grated
4 celery sticks, chopped
1 crisp dessert apple, cored and chopped
50g (2oz) seedless raisins
50g (2oz) cashew nuts, roasted
juice of ½ lemon
3 tablespoons Greek-style yogurt
salt and freshly ground black pepper

Mix the vegetables, fruit and nuts in a large salad bowl.

Stir the lemon juice and salt and pepper into the yogurt then toss the salad in the dressing.

Cover and chill until required.

creamy mustard potato salad

The first new potatoes of the season are a real treat. Use a variety such as Pink Fir Apple or Anya for an excellent potato salad.

30 mins
prep & cook time

serves 6

149 cals
per serving

7g fat
per serving

750g (1¹/₂lb) new potatoes
3 tablespoons mayonnaise
1 tablespoon Dijon mustard
20g (³/₄oz) fresh mint leaves, chopped
100g (3¹/₂oz) wild rocket
salt and freshly ground black pepper

Cook the potatoes in lightly salted boiling water for approximately 20 minutes or until just tender.

Drain and allow to cool slightly.

Blend together the mayonnaise, mustard, most of the mint and plenty of seasoning to taste.

Toss the warm potatoes in the mayonnaise mixture and serve warm, sprinkled with the remaining chopped mint.

Delicious served on a bed of wild rocket leaves as an accompaniment to poultry or meat.

minted runner beans

The crispy bacon gives runner beans a glorious zing and makes a change from plain boiled.

30 mins
prep & cook time

serves 4

147 cals
per serving

12g fat
per serving

175g (6oz) runner beans, stringed and sliced in thick chunks
2 tablespoons mint jelly
4 rashers rindless streaky bacon, grilled until crisp
salt and freshly ground black pepper

Cook the beans for 5-6 minutes in a pan of lightly salted boiling water, then drain well and set aside.

Gently warm the mint jelly, stir in the bacon and beans, and season to taste. Serve immediately.

bubble and squeak

The recipe for bubble and squeak is over 200 years old; it was made on Monday evenings to use up the vegetables left-over from Sunday lunch. Cooking cabbage squeaks in the pan!

30 mins prep & cook time

serves 4

247 cals per serving

14g fat per serving

500g (1lb) potatoes, peeled and boiled
50g (2oz) butter
100g (3¹/₂oz) bacon
250g (8oz) cabbage or Brussels sprouts,
   cooked and chopped
1 tablespoon chopped parsley
3 tablespoons oil
salt and freshly ground black pepper

Mash the potatoes with the butter and season.

Fry the bacon until crispy, crumble and stir into the mash with the cabbage or Brussels sprouts and parsley.

Shape the potato mix into 4 rounds and flatten slightly with the palm of your hand.

Heat the oil in a frying pan and fry the cakes for 4 minutes on each side, or until golden.

Serve with cold meat, vine or cherry tomatoes and tomato chutney.

fruity red cabbage

A great winter vegetable dish – warming and spicy flavours mingle to create a luscious end result.

30 mins		109 cals	2g fat
prep & cook time	serves 6-8	per serving	per serving

1kg (2lb) red cabbage, shredded
500g (1lb) red onions, finely sliced
500g (1lb) cooking apples, peeled, cored
  and sliced
2 cloves garlic, finely chopped
1 teaspoon freshly grated nutmeg
1/2 teaspoon ground cinnamon
3 tablespoons soft brown sugar
4 tablespoons red wine vinegar
20g (3/4oz) butter, cut into small pieces
salt and freshly ground black pepper

In a large flameproof casserole, arrange a layer of shredded cabbage, season, then add a layer of onion and apple.

In a small bowl, mix together the garlic, nutmeg, cinnamon and sugar. Sprinkle a little of this mixture over the top of the apples.

Continue with these alternating layers of cabbage, onion, apple and spice mixture, until all the ingredients are used.

Pour over the vinegar and dot the surface with the small pieces of butter. Cover with a well fitting lid or foil and cook over a low heat for 1 hour, stirring occasionally.

bacon and cabbage with crispy onions

A good accompaniment to pork, but just as delicious eaten for lunch with warm crusty bread.

20 mins		452 cals	28g fat
prep & cook time	serves 2	per serving	per serving

25g (1oz) butter
1 tablespoon oil
4 rashers rindless smoked streaky bacon, cut into pieces
150g (5oz) spring greens
1 tablespoon crispy onion topping

Heat the butter and oil in a large frying pan or wok, add the bacon and stir-fry for 3-4 minutes.

Add the spring greens and stir-fry for a further 2-3 minutes. Sprinkle over the crispy onion topping and serve.

COOK'S TIP
Replace the crispy onion topping with croûtons or toasted breadcrumbs.

cheesy kale gratin

(*right*)

Don't overcook this under-rated vegetable – you don't want to lose its fantastic green colour.

30 mins		**192 cals**	**11g fat**
prep & cook time	serves 4-6	per serving	per serving

250g (8oz) kale, stalks removed and finely shredded
25g (1oz) butter
25g (1oz) plain flour
450ml (3/4 pint) full fat milk
125g (4oz) goats' cheese, crumbled
1/2 teaspoon mustard powder
75g (3oz) fresh white breadcrumbs
1 tablespoon caraway seeds
salt and freshly ground black pepper

Preheat the oven to 190°C/375°F/gas mark 5. Plunge the kale into boiling water for 30-60 seconds, then refresh under cold water. Put to one side.

Melt the butter in a saucepan, stir in the flour and cook for 1-2 minutes. Remove the pan from the heat and gradually blend in the milk, stirring well. Place back on the heat and bring gently to the boil, stirring continuously until thickened and smooth. Add the cheese, mustard powder, salt and freshly ground black pepper, and mix well.

Place the kale in an ovenproof dish, then spoon over the sauce. Combine the breadcrumbs and caraway seeds, then spread evenly over the surface. Bake in the oven for 20-25 minutes or until the topping is golden brown.

creamed leeks

A delicious dish made from on of the Welsh national emblems

30 mins		**252 cals**	**24g fat**
prep & cook time	serves 1	per serving	per serving

15g (3/4 oz) butter
1 leek, cleaned and sliced
2 tablespoons crème fraîche
salt and freshly ground black pepper

Heat the butter and fry the leek until it just begins to colour.

Mix in the crème fraîche, season and heat through before serving.

COOK'S TIP
Use low-fat crème fraîche for a lower-fat alternative.

bacon and chestnut sprouts

A Christmas dish that's as traditional as red telephone boxes!

30 mins
prep & cook time

serves 4

280 cals
per serving

17g fat
per serving

375g (12oz) Brussels sprouts, trimmed
25g (1oz) butter
4 rashers rindless smoked streaky bacon, chopped
200g (7oz) cooked and peeled chestnuts, halved
salt and freshly ground black pepper

Place the Brussels sprouts in a large pan of boiling water and cook for 5-8 minutes until just tender.

Melt the butter in a large frying pan and add the bacon. Fry until crispy.

Add the chestnuts and drained sprouts and cook for a further minute, mixing well. Season to taste.

COOK'S TIP
You can cook your own chestnuts from scratch, but vacuum-packed chestnuts are easily available now and are just as good.

beetroot and horseradish gratin

Rediscover the earthy, nutty taste of an old favourite.

45 mins
prep & cook time

serves 4-6

241 cals
per serving

11g fat
per serving

50g (2oz) butter
50g (2oz) plain flour
450ml (³/4 pint) milk
2 tablespoons crème fraîche
3 tablespoons horseradish sauce
300g (10oz) cooked beetroot, chopped into
   large pieces
100g (3¹/2oz) fresh white or brown
   breadcrumbs
2 tablespoons freshly grated Parmesan
   cheese
salt and freshly ground black pepper

Preheat the oven to 200°C/400°F/gas mark 6.

To make the sauce, melt the butter in a saucepan, add the flour and mix to a smooth paste. Cook for 1-2 minutes, stirring continously.

Remove the saucepan from the heat and gradually blend in the milk. Return to the heat and bring gently to the boil, stirring continuously until the sauce thickens.

Stir in the crème fraîche, horseradish sauce and season with salt and pepper.

Place the beetroot chunks in an ovenproof dis● and pour over the sauce.

Sprinkle the breadcrumbs and Parmesan over the top and bake for 25-30 minutes or until th● top is golden brown.

COOK'S TIP
If you buy ready-cooked beetroot, make sur●
you buy the plainly cooked variety, rather
than the sort that is packed in vinegar.

To cook your own beetroot, trim off the top
leaves, leaving a small stump, and keep the
root on. Wash the mud off, being careful not
break the skins, and boil whole in salted wat●
for 30 minutes to 2 hours, depending on siz●
and age of the beets.

The tops of young beetroots make an
excellent addition to a green salad and have
very pretty vein markings on the leaves.

celery, pear and stilton crumble bake

A great combination of tastes and textures makes a perfect side dish or light lunch.

45 mins
prep & cook time

serves 4-6

186 cals
per serving

12g fat
per serving

1 head celery, trimmed, peeled and cut into 5cm (2in) pieces
3 comice pears, peeled, cored and cut into 2cm (³/₄in) wedges
284ml (10fl oz) pot single cream
50g (2oz) Stilton cheese, crumbled
50g (2oz) wholemeal breadcrumbs
salt and freshly ground black pepper

Preheat oven to 200°C/400°F/gas mark 6.

Blanch the celery in boiling water for 2-3 minutes and refresh under cold running water. Layer the celery and pear in a suitable size ovenproof dish. Pour over the cream and season with salt and freshly ground black pepper.

Dot with the Stilton cheese and liberally sprinkle over the breadcrumbs.

Place in the oven and bake for 30 minutes or until the crumb topping is golden brown.

cheese and chive soufflé jackets

The skins of baked potatoes contain all the vitamins. These make good warming fare.

2 hrs
prep & cook time

serves 4

360 cals
per serving

15g fat
per serving

4 medium baking potatoes, pricked
25g (1oz) butter
100ml (3¹/₂oz) milk, warmed
100g (3¹/₂oz) grated Cheddar cheese
¹/₂ small pot chives
4 egg whites

Preheat the oven to 200°C/400°F/gas mark 6.

Place the potatoes on a baking sheet and cook for 1¹/₂ hours until soft.

Remove from the oven, cut in half and scoop out the potato into a bowl. Combine with the butter and milk to achieve a smooth creamy mash. Stir in the cheese and chives.

Whisk the egg whites in a bowl until they form soft peaks. Fold into the mashed potato and spoon back into the potato skins.

Return to the oven and cook for 10-15 minutes or until golden brown and well risen. Delicious served with a crisp watercress salad.

jacket chips with tartare-style sauce

Keep on the jackets for extra crunch and goodness!

30 mins		**391** cals	**21g** fat
prep & cook time	serves 4-6	per serving	per serving

1.5kg (3½lb) Maris Piper potatoes,
  scrubbed and dried
vegetable oil, for deep-fat frying

For the sauce:
250ml (8fl oz) mayonnaise
50g (2oz) capers, drained well and chopped
50g (2oz) gherkins, drained well and chopped
a little flaked sea salt, to taste
freshly ground black pepper, to taste

Cut the potatoes into into 1cm (½in) thick slices, then cut again to give long chips approximately 1cm (½in) thick and 7cm (3in) long.

Blanch the chips in boiling water for 3-4 minutes. Drain the chips well on a single layer of kitchen paper until dry to the touch.

Heat the oil for deep-fat frying to 190ºC/375ºF and cook the chips until golden brown and crispy. Drain well and sprinkle with salt. Keep hot.

Mix all the remaining ingredients together to make the sauce. Season to taste. Serve with the chips.

spiced parsnips

Cinnamon and sugar make a gorgeous coating for parsnips.

30 mins		**253** cals	**12**g fat
prep & cook time	serves 4	per serving	per serving

750g (1¹/₂lb) frozen baby parsnips
50g (2oz) butter, melted or oil
3 tablespoons soft brown sugar
1 teaspoon ground cinnamon
1 teaspoon grated lemon zest

Preheat the oven to 220°C/425°F/gas mark 7.

Cook the parsnips in boiling water for 2 minutes, then drain and toss in the melted butter or oil.

Mix together the sugar, cinnamon and lemon zest.

Roll the buttered parsnips in the sugar mixture and bake in the oven for 20 minutes.

glazed carrots

Delicious sweet-sour flavours come through here.

30 mins
prep & cook time

serves 2

170 cals
per serving

13g fat
per serving

200g (7oz) baby carrots
4 tablespoons orange juice
25g (1oz) butter
2 teaspoons sugar

Put all the ingredients in a small saucepan and add just enough water to cover.

Bring to the boil, cover and simmer for 15–20 minutes until the carrots are tender and the water has evaporated.

Watch closely towards the end of cooking, and shake the pan occasionally to prevent the carrots sticking.

creamy spiced swede purée

The ginger gives this much neglected vegetable a delicious zing. Good with plain meats.

 45 mins prep & cook time

 serves 4

 59 cals per serving

 3g fat per serving

1 swede, peeled and cut into 1cm (½in) dice
20g (¾ oz) butter
½ teaspoon ground ginger
pinch of finely grated nutmeg
2 tablespoons crème fraîche, plus extra, to garnish
1 tablespoon coarsely chopped flat-leaf parsley
salt and freshly ground black pepper

Cook the diced swede in boiling salted water for 20-30 minutes or until very tender.

Drain the swede well and purée in a food processor or liquidiser until smooth. For a very fine texture press the purée through a sieve.

Transfer the mixture to a clean saucepan. Stir in the butter and spices and add salt and pepper to taste. Gently heat through.

Stir in the crème fraîche and pile the mixture into a warm serving dish. Garnish with a swirl of crème fraîche, a sprinkle of flat-leaf parsley and some freshly ground black pepper.

tangy roast roots with chestnuts

A long cooking time transforms crunchy vegetables into meltingly soft mouthfuls.

1 hr		252 cals	13g fat
prep & cook time	serves 4	per serving	per serving

1 parsnip, chopped
1 leek, trimmed and chopped
10g (¹/₃oz) fresh thyme, leaves only
50g (2oz) butter
2 carrots, diced
200g (7oz) chestnuts, cooked and peeled
¹/₂ Savoy cabbage, shredded
1 tablespoon Seville orange marmalade
¹/₂ chicken stock cube made up with 150ml
  (¹/₄ pint) boiling water
salt and freshly ground black pepper

Preheat the oven to 180°C/350°F/gas mark 4.

Place the parsnip and leek in a roasting tin, add the thyme and seasoning. Dot with butter and cook in the preheated oven for 10 minutes, stirring once.

Add the carrots and cook for a further 30 minutes, until just tender.

Add the chestnuts, cabbage, marmalade and chicken stock and cook for a further 10 minutes. Serve hot.

puddings

apple syllabub

A modern version of a dessert that dates back to Elizabethan times. Originally made with wine or beer, 'bub' is Old English slang for a bubbling drink.

1½ hrs
prep & cook time

serves 6

299 cals
per serving

23g fat
per serving

3 Golden Delicious apples, peeled, cored and chopped
2 tablespoons water
1 tablespoon caster sugar
150ml (5fl oz) sweet white wine
zest and juice of 1 lemon
50g (2oz) caster sugar
300ml (10fl oz) double cream
fresh mint sprigs
apple slices

Place the chopped apples, water and sugar in a saucepan, cover and cook for 8-10 minutes or until soft. Allow to cool.

Place the wine, lemon zest and juice, sugar and cream in a bowl and whisk until the mixture holds its shape.

Carefully fold in the apple purée and spoon into 6 tall glasses.

Allow to chill for 1-2 hours, then decorate with the mint and apple slices.

fresh fruit jelly

A beautiful dessert that's perfect for a summer celebration.

3½ hrs
prep & cook time

serves 4

110 cals
per serving

1g fat
per serving

600ml (1 pint) white grape or apple juice
4 teaspoons powdered gelatine
50g (2oz) white grapes, halved and deseeded
50g (2oz) black grapes, halved and deseeded
50g (2oz) strawberries, washed and quartered
50g (2oz) blueberries, washed

Put 5 tablespoons of the fruit juice in a small saucepan. Slowly sprinkle the gelatine over the top, making sure that it is completely absorbed by the liquid and that there are no dry patches. Avoid stirring if possible. Set aside to 'sponge' for at least 5 minutes.

Put the saucepan over a low heat and allow the gelatine to melt, without boiling, until the liquid is clear and not cloudy.

Heat the remaining fruit juice for 1 minute in a large saucepan. Stir the dissolved gelatine into the mixture and leave to stand for 15 minutes to cool.

Mix the fruits together and pile into a large serving bowl of 1 litre (1³/4 pint) capacity. Pour the cool fruit liquid over the top. Cover and chill for 3-4 hours until the jelly is completely set.

COOK'S TIP
You can use orange juice as an alternative, but a clear jelly shows the fruit off best.

lemon pancakes

A Shrove Tuesday tradition you can enjoy all year.

prep & cook time	makes 8-10 pancakes	per serving	per serving

125g (4oz) plain flour
pinch of salt
1 egg
300ml (1/2 pint) milk
oil, for frying

To serve:
juice of 1 lemon
sugar to taste
lemon twists

Sift the flour and salt into a bowl. Add the egg and gradually beat in half the milk. Add the remaining milk and beat until smooth.

Lightly oil a frying pan and place over a moderate heat. Pour in just enough batter to cover the base of the pan. Cook until the underside is golden, then turn and cook the other side. Cool on a wire rack. Repeat with the remaining batter.

To serve, sprinkle with lemon juice, roll up and top with sugar and lemon twists.

To freeze, stack the pancakes with greaseproof paper between each one. Place the pile in a polythene bag. Seal, label and freeze.

To serve, thaw the wrapped pile at room temperature for 2-3 hours, or remove individual pancakes as needed and thaw for 15-20 minutes.

Unwrap the the pile and reheat in a moderately hot oven, 190°C/375°F/gas mark 5, for 20-30 minutes.

Alternatively, reheat individual pancakes in a lightly greased hot frying pan for about 3 minutes on each side.

COOK'S TIP
You can use the same batter to make savour pancakes. It is a very useful way to use up left-over chicken or turkey, in a sauce made with onions, mushrooms and cream.

spiced scones with fruit compôte

A summer tradition, scones are the perfect teatime treat.

40 mins
prep & cook time

makes 16 scones

478 cals
per serving

25g fat
per serving

250ml (8fl oz) low-fat natural yogurt
100ml (3¹/₂fl oz) milk (plus 2 tablespoons
   for the glaze)
75g (3oz) clear honey
625g (1¹/₄lb) plain flour
1¹/₂ teaspoons baking powder
1¹/₂ teaspoons caster sugar
1 teaspoon salt
1 teaspoon ground cinnamon
125g (4oz) butter, cut into small pieces
1 egg yolk mixed with 2 tablespoons milk

250g (8oz) apricot and prune compôte
200ml (7fl oz) crème fraîche

Preheat the oven to 200°C/400°F/gas mark 6.

Combine the yogurt, milk and honey in a jug.

In a bowl, mix together the plain flour, baking
powder, sugar, salt and ground cinnamon.

Add the butter and rub into the dry ingredients
until the mixture resembles fine breadcrumbs.
Make a well in the centre of the dry ingredients,
then gradually mix in the yogurt, milk and honey
until it forms a ball.

Turn the dough onto a lightly floured surface
and roll to a thickness of 2cm (³/₄in). Cut the
dough into rounds using a 7cm (3in) pastry
cutter, re-rolling as necessary to achieve a total
of 16 scones.

Place the scones on two non-stick baking trays
5cm (2in) apart. Glaze with the combined egg
yolk and milk, place in the oven and cook for 15
minutes or until golden brown.

Serve with the compôte and creme fraîche.

plum crumble

It seems that crumbles date from the Second World War - a sweeter alternative to pastry.

45 mins — prep & cook time

serves 4

295 cals — per serving

11g fat — per serving

500g (1lb) plums, halved and stoned
125g (4oz) plain wholemeal flour
50g (2oz) butter or margarine
50g (2oz) caster sugar
low-fat natural yogurt or fromage frais, to
   serve

Preheat the oven to 190°C/375 °F/gas mark 5.

Place the fruit in a deep ovenproof dish and add 1 tablespoon water.

Put the flour in a mixing bowl, add the butter or margarine and rub it in with your fingertips until the mixture resembles fine breadcrumbs. Stir in the sugar, sprinkle the crumble mixture over the top of the fruit and bake in the oven for 25-30 minutes.

Serve hot with yogurt or fromage frais.

COOK'S TIP
Replace the plums with other fruit: rhubarb, berries, apples or even tinned apricots.

apple and marmalade custard pudding

The tartness of good marmalade perfectly complements apples.

1½ hrs		**321 cals**	**13g fat**
prep & cook time	serves 8-10	per serving	per serving

20g (³/₄oz) unsalted butter
4 dessert apples, peeled, cored and roughly chopped
½ teaspoon ground cinnamon
1 litre (1³/₄ pints) longlife custard
2 x Madeira cakes, cut into slices 1cm (½in) thick
50g (2oz) orange marmalade

Preheat the oven to 190ºC/375ºF/gas mark 5.

Place a saucepan over a moderate heat. Add the butter, apples and cinnamon and cook gently for 3-4 minutes.

Pour the custard into the saucepan and heat it through gently, stirring occasionally. Remove from the heat.

Lay half the cake slices in a 1 litre (1³/₄pint) ovenproof dish and pour over the apple custard.

Spread the marmalade over the remaining cake slices and cut each piece in half, diagonally. Lay the slices over the apple custard, marmalade side up.

Cover the dish with foil. Place on a baking sheet and bake in the preheated oven for 50 minutes.

Heat a grill to a hot setting. When the pudding cooked, place under the hot grill for 1 minute to colour the surface.

Serve hot or cold with cream or ice cream.

golden bramley pie

The king of cooking apples has its origins in 1809 when a Mr Bramley discovered these apples growing in his garden.

| prep & cook time | serves 4-6 | 394 cals per serving | 18g fat per serving |

375g (12oz) ready-to roll shortcrust pastry
1 tablespoon plain flour
2 large Bramley apples, peeled, cored and
   thinly sliced
50g (2oz) demerara sugar
½ teaspoon ground cinnamon
50g (2oz) sultanas
50g (2oz) demerara sugar

Preheat the oven to 200°C/400°F/gas mark 6.

Roll out two-thirds of the pastry to a thickness of 5mm (¼in) in thickness. Use to line a 18cm (7in) flan tin. Sprinkle the base of the pastry with the flour.

Place the apple, sugar, cinnamon and sultanas in a bowl and combine. Layer into the base of the pastry case.

Sprinkle the demerara sugar for the topping onto a work surface. Roll out the remaining pastry over the sugar. Turn over and roll again until a thickness of 5mm (¼in) is achieved.

Cut into 10 strips, each 1cm (½in) in width and of varying lengths to fit the tin.

Twist each strip once or twice and place over the

apple filling in neat lines, pressing the end of th twist to the pastry base. Flute the edges of the pie.

Place on a baking tray and cook for 30-35 minutes, until golden brown. If it starts to brow too quickly, cover with foil.

Serve hot or cold with cream or ice cream.

COOK'S TIP
Bramley's Seedlings keep their shape well during cooking and have one of the highest vitamin C contents of cooking varieties. It is also the apple sold in greatest quantity because it stores so well.

parkin

This sticky cake is now as much a part of Bonfire Night as Guy Fawkes himself.

prep & cook time	serves 12	per serving	per serving
1 hr		344 cals	14g fat

175g (6oz) golden syrup
100g (3¹/₂oz) black treacle
75g (3oz) light muscovado sugar
175g (6oz) unsalted butter
200g (7oz) oatmeal
250g (8oz) plain flour
1 teaspoon ground ginger
2 teaspoons bicarbonate of soda
1 egg beaten with 3 tablespoons milk

Preheat the oven to 170°C/325°F/gas mark 3. Line a 23cm (9in) square tin with parchment paper, including the sides.

Put the syrup, treacle, sugar and butter in a small saucepan and dissolve together. Put to one side when well mixed.

Mix together the oatmeal, flour, ginger and bicarbonate of soda and stir into the syrup, followed by the egg.

Pour into the prepared tin and bake for 1 hour, or until an inserted skewer comes out clean.

Transfer to a wire rack, remove the paper and allow to cool. Cut into 12 pieces.

chocolate bread-and-butter pudding

Brioche, panettone and even slices of plain cake can be used in this nostalgic pudding. Bread and butter pudding has been made since medieval times.

prep & cook time	serves 4-6	per serving	per serving
1 hr		742 cals	43g fat

600ml (1 pint) milk
284ml (10fl oz) pot double cream
4 whole eggs plus 4 egg yolks
125g (4oz) caster sugar
few drops vanilla extract
1/2 baguette, cut into slices
50g (2oz) sultanas
50g (2oz) plain chocolate, roughly chopped
50g (2oz) butter, melted
4 tablespoons apricot jam
2 tablespoons orange juice

Preheat the oven to 190°C/375°F/gas mark 5. You will need an ovenproof dish 18cm (7in) long and 4cm (1³/₄in) deep.

In a medium-size saucepan bring the milk and the double cream to the boil over a moderate heat.

Meanwhile mix together in a bowl the whole eggs, egg yolks and caster sugar. Pour over the milk and cream mixture, stir well to combine, then strain into a jug, adding the vanilla extract.

Layer half of the sliced baguette in the bottom of the ovenproof dish, and scatter over the sultanas and chocolate.

Dip the remaining slices of bread in the melted butter and lay them on top of the sultanas. Pour over the custard mixture and leave to soak for 30 minutes, pushing the bread beneath the surface of the custard.

Place the dish in a bain-marie (a roasting tin containing hot water to reach to halfway up the sides of the ovenproof dish). Bake the pudding for 1 hour until golden brown.

In a small saucepan heat together the apricot jam and orange juice. Brush liberally over the bread-and-butter pudding and serve immediately.

index